II

LONG, WHITISH CLOUDLAND

SIR HARRY LOGGAT SCOTT

a LIST *of*
ATTRACTIONS
along with
ACCOMPANYING PAGINATION:

V

to our world's most prolific author of postal artworks:

On Jay, Lain-a-Lay—

in addition to Kiwi Country's convivial souls,

whom this troubadour portrays

jubilantly, with honor...

I

MĀORILAND

I.I) It was magic, moving to Māoriland:

I.II) It was a plan in which I had no hand.

I.III) As a proudly lay ornithologist,

I.IV) I was always—from infancy—hoping

I.V) To find kiwi birds. An apologist

I.VI) For animals, I was daily moping

I.VII) About how poorly humans took caring

I.VIII) Of unusual organisms. So,

I.IX) In a ridiculously apt pairing

I.X) Of circumstantial acts, I got to go.

II.I) I got to inhabit this Land of Long,

II.II) Whitish Clouds, in our world's South Pacific,

II.III) Down across from Australia. It's wrong,

II.IV) Though, to call this land an honorific

II.V) That can't distinguish Country Kangaroo

II.VI) From that Ti-Ri-Ti of Waitangi. Too,

II.VII) Such islands no coronavirus had,

II.VIII) Which was driving sad California mad,

II.IX) In addition to all our world's nations,

II.X) From Finnish Nova Scotians to Haitians.

III.I) Whilst coronavirus was occurring,

III.II) Australasia simply shut off all flights

III.III) From cosmopolitan airports. Purring

III.IV) Was Post-Industrialization: Lights,

III.V) Filming, Action! Aunty Jacinda built—

III.VI) For mass-quarantining—a ministry

III.VII) That, from abroad, brought in souls
>   —to full tilt—

III.VIII) Via viral-proof ways. An industry

III.IX) To hold such souls whilst in lockdown
>   sprung up

III.X) As instantly as Starbucks java cup.

IV.I) That August, post-high school graduation—

IV.II) Which was, owing to masks, had thru driving—

IV.III) I got across Harry Truman's nation,

IV.IV) Mowing lawns—into which I was diving—

IV.V) Of small-town Ohio, by plains of corn,

IV.VI) For living in Hollywood now was shorn.

IV.VII) Riots that May had to my pupils shown

IV.VIII) How calm in California was on loan;

IV.IX) Policing local politicians sought

IV.X) To limit—just as many shops got shot.

V.I) In this City of Lost, Angsty Cupids,

V.II) I would walk for hours—days—atop gross glass

V.III) That burst from rainbow graffiti. For kids,

V.IV) Such nightmarish roads can't possibly pass.

V.V) Against such crazy kristallnachts I fought

V.VI) By voting with my body; Ohio

V.VII) Was amply placid. As soon as I caught,

V.VIII) Though, a spot for moving out of this low,

V.IX) To a magical island chain away,

V.X) Far from all looting—it was a grand day.

VI.I) That is how I found my body flying

VI.II) On an aircraft from LAX airport

VI.III) Atop our Pacific, although dying

VI.IV) Was my aorta, in which my soul's fort

VI.V) Was falling apart, for I was missing

VI.VI) Many a fantasy that I had wrought,

VI.VII) But could not now vivify. Pain was bought—

VI.VIII) As my old imagination, hissing

VI.IX) As if an asp, had again all to start:

VI.X) For Māoriland, normalcy had to part.

VII.I) As glad as I was Auckland-wards to go,

VII.II) Abandoning family and pals was far

VII.III) From fun, a cirrus-stratus joy sub-par,

VII.IV) In particular having not to know

VII.V) At what point I, from abroad, would run back.

VII.VI) Cross-cultural notions I did not lack,

VII.VII) But—at this point in history—moving

VII.VIII) Across nations was wondrously jarring:

VII.IX) To stop viral growth, policy barring

VII.X) Immigration was wrought, if not proving.

VIII.I) Ao-Ta-Ya-Ro-A, this Māori nation—

VIII.II) Of Pavlova tart's first innovation—

VIII.III) Forms soil from islands chains manifold;

VIII.IV) South Alps cash banks with

Pounamu and Gold.

VIII.V) That North Island is Maui's Ika Fish

VIII.VI) Into which Gondor, Rhovanion squish;

VIII.VII) That South Island Tay Waipounamu rolls

VIII.VIII) On Forodwaith wizardry's rippling knolls;

VIII.IX) Kakapo's misty mountains mystify;

VIII.X) Bliss history Kiwi crowns justify.

IX.I) But such is how magic will warmly work.

IX.II) Thus, atop Samoa coconut coasts—

IX.III) Upon which colonialism lurks—

IX.IV) I was sobbing in an aircraft, with hosts—

IX.V) For whom but thirty spots had a body—

IX.VI) Who brought my first drink,

                which was not shoddy.

IX.VII) Faithfully following Washington's laws,

IX.VIII) I—as a young inhabitant—did not

IX.IX) At any point drink in that land of <u>Jaws</u>

IX.X) And <u>Star Wars</u>; alcohol was bad, I thought.

X.I) "Do you want a drink?"—this host inquiring.

X.II) "What?" "I can pour pinot noir, chardonnay…"

X.III) —Acting as if on a Bahaman cay!

X.IV) "No thank you," I fast said, also tiring

X.V) In what was now night. That following day:

X.VI) "You know that I'm just six plus six plus six

X.VII) Autumns old?"—out of which our host

       got kicks.

X.VIII) "Kiwi customs can apply now, okay?"

X.IX) That Marlborough pinot noir was tasty;

X.X) Am glad that growing up was not hasty.

XIX

II

AUCKLAND TĀMAKI-MAKAU-RAU

I.I) Flying thru fog from our South Spring's first night,

I.II) Atop Tāmaki-Makau-Rau's bright light,

I.III) Past grassy hillocks, plus volcanic shoals,

I.IV) Salty pupils had burnt up most cool coals.

I.V) Dorothy's odd city of Oz glows with

I.VI) Colours that shroud Hauraki Gulf in myth:

I.VII) Atop Mount Rangitoto's rim run rains,

I.VIII) Alighting arcs from that Ark of Noah's—

I.IX) Proof of God—across this Land of Moas,

I.X) All of whom—summiting alps—pull down pains.

II.I) Upon Auckland Airport's tarmac at dawn—

II.II) Just prior to Spring's first shook shafts of sun—

II.III) That Hauraki Gulf looks as if a con,

II.IV) Brimming with cyan that outcrops shan't shun,

II.V) In glory of glowing opals and golds

II.VI) Which go twinkling in South Pacific calm,

II.VII) For ultra-indigo rays of which, balm—

II.VIII) Upon skin—a chilly, sticky play holds.

II.IX) Smokily suffocating chaparral

II.X) Could not look similar to this at all.

III.I) Inland from Alta California's coast

III.II) Tons of months prior to Autumn had brought—

III.III) Back to blazing—many a flaming ghost,

III.IV) Who would cough gray,

                pinkish hazings that caught

III.V) Hollywood by storm, many a lung torn

III.VI) Throughout filmy dazings, in which was born

III.VII) Hardly any hoping for survival

III.VIII) In civic harmony. An arrival,

III.IX) Thus, to this Trans-Tasman isthmus shocks

III.X) Any aorta who pumps polar locks.

IV.I) Tāmaki-Makau-Rau, Isthmus of a,

IV.II) Myths say, Thousand Loving Souls—

who can't pay

IV.III) Thoughts worth rubbish to global goings-on—

IV.IV) Fights against turning into paltry pawn.

IV.V) Plus, this Quasi-British city will not

IV.VI) Allow most inhabitants to fall poor:

IV.VII) For All-Blacks winning rugby, Kiwis roar.

IV.VIII) Thanks to sound socialism, any pot

IV.IX) Holds poultry, possibly kai moana,

IV.X) Tasting distinct from Brazil's piranha.

V.I) Arising from Manukau at sunlight,

V.II) Atop Taranaki pulling snow tight,

V.III) Our aircraft was gliding on Maui's fish,

V.IV) Gazing at wondrous Waikato. My wish—

V.V) Down to Pavlova's origin looking—

V.VI) Was to know Māoriland. Notions cooking

V.VII) In hippocampus curiosity

V.VIII) Rip past practical animosity

V.IX) Against voyaging into grand unknown:

V.X) Manawatu's magic dairy was shown.

VI.I) Island chains drip topaz sub-tropical;

VI.II) Sub-antarctic (bark, tick); sub-optical

VI.III) Conditions from which to look at

Mount Doom:

VI.IV) Tongariro Volcano's lava tomb.

VI.V) South of Taupō-Moana, gushing gloom

VI.VI) Zips thru North Island's low-rain, dry crossing,

VI.VII) Around which Australasian flora bloom:

VI.VIII) Houpara, Poroporo bush tossing.

VI.IX) Kiwi wool socks—of which I had no pair—

VI.X) Would work aptly in frigid, racing air.

VII.I) Moving up against mad Marlborough Sounds,

VII.II) Which push out—magnanimously in mounds—

VII.III) Of what was long ago a thalassic

VII.IV) Mammal hunting hub: Cook Strait, triassic

VII.V) In rock origin, but truly as young

VII.VI) As cold capitalism's swan song sung

VII.VII) To ginormous milk-animals di mar,

VII.VIII) On which Captain Ahab staid far off par.

VII.IX) Across from Picton, Port Whaling Station

VII.X) Took tons of cuddly cubs from lactation.

VIII.I) From Tāmaki-Makau-Rau took our flight

VIII.II) To Port Nicholson. Political blight

VIII.III) Pounds so poor in this capital city,

VIII.IV) That locals call it Wailing-Town (pity)—

VIII.V) Or Wailington, from which port did abort

VIII.VI) Māori colonists to Chatham Islands.

VIII.VII) Spiritually similar import

VIII.VIII) Looks to Cymric, Pictish, Manx

wool-highlands:

VIII.IX) Bicultural constitutionally;

VIII.X) Brit-Māori mix attitudinally.

IX.I) Our day out of quarantining shook,

IX.II) All lissom body parts with joy. It took

IX.III) Six plus two plus six nights of staying put

IX.IV) In a singular room, but our last hook

IX.V) Could cook out any sort of sultry soot,

IX.VI) At additional waiting hours for which

IX.VII) I could not bring puny pupils to look.

IX.VIII) Dousing diaphanous lockdown with pitch,

IX.IX) Our group got to—upon confirmation—

IX.X) Sprint into vibrant, no-virus nation.

X.I) Hopping outdoors—sunny!—was outstanding,

X.II) Awash onto panoramic landing—

X.III) In vivid airport full of crowds sans masks—

X.IV) I could go mingling, in hand with tall tasks,

X.V) A singular goal of which was to walk,

X.VI) About all my plans for which I would talk,

X.VII) Fast flying back to that City of Sails,

X.VIII) In which kids quickly find Tui-bird tails

X.IX) Around, across this volcanic isthmus

X.X) Of Auckland—as amazing as Christmas.

XXX

XXXI

III

RANGITOTO, MOTU-TABOO

I.I) Singular Bush Hill, capping Cornwall Park,

I.II) For Auckland climbs languorous landmark,

I.III) Atop Royal Oak, Oranga, just south

I.IV) Of Mount Hobson, Maungawhau,

Mount Saint John,

I.V) Away from Puponga Point, harbour mouth,

I.VI) Rising from many a suburban lawn

I.VII) In Kiwi Country's most ginormous town

I.VIII) Of Otahuhu, Otara, Southdown.

I.IX) Right across Maui's Fish, Auckland's map mills,

I.X) Flowing thru farmland, à la tidal twills.

II.I) Waita-Carry Mountains mould Muriwai

II.II) By Pillow Lava Point, south of Hwa-Pai;

II.III) Otakamiro, Bartrum Bays gush forth

II.IV) By wavy Piha's Lion Rock, just north

II.V) Of famous swim-guards: Manukau Harbour.

II.VI) Hui-a Dams control brooks by Titirangi,

II.VII) Parau, by which grows many an arbor,

II.VIII) In thick, prickly bush. Go to a hangi

II.IX) For rough, smoky kai-carrots burnt in dirt

II.X) By Waitaruan woods—It can't hurt!

III.I) Auckland's North Shoring holds Takapuna,

III.II) Which can cook—of coursing—tasty tuna.

III.III) Marlborough, Milford, Highbury, Vauxhall

III.IV) To Sunnynook's Rahopara Point fall.

III.V) Musical Mairangi Bay's Maroon Bluff—

III.VI) On top of which many mansions off-cuff

III.VII) Talk Afrikaans—mould coasts right across

III.VIII) From Rangitoto's baby volcano

III.IX) As young as Istanbul, as if a cross

III.X) Halving Hauraki (to which don't say no).

IV.I) Bastion Point—by Mission, Okahu Bays,

IV.II) Along which you may walk for stunning days—

IV.III) Floats south of Rangitoto's Flax Point, and—

IV.IV) I should add—across that Island of Brown's,

IV.V) Around which many a quick kayak hounds,

IV.VI) Though will in Half-Moon/Wai-o-Taiki land.

IV.VII) North of Saint John's, Kohimarama cools

IV.VIII) Winds coming from holy Motu-Taboo:

IV.IX) Rubbing Rangitoto, this outcrop fools

IV.X) Albatross down Bay Waikalabubu.

V.I) Two months prior to Kamala Harris

V.II) In January: I, as if Paris,

V.III) Ran off to Motu-Taboo for my Troy,

V.IV) Running away from notifications—

V.V) About which my soul was totally coy—

V.VI) On John Jay's nation. Trump's polling
                    —too tight—

V.VII) Could tally for days. Ramifications:

V.VIII) I had to part from civilization

V.IX) To rural wilds without digital light,

V.X) So I had not to know quick causation.

VI.I) For days, thus, Motu-Taboo I did tramp—

VI.II) Post All-Hallow's night—so that I could wait,

VI.III) Whilst studying Swahili/stringing bait,

VI.IV) For all voting counts to finish. First camp:

VI.V) Put up nylon tipi in yowling rain,

VI.VI) Hours past sundown in Islington Bay. Gain:

VI.VII) I now know how important is a watch,

VI.VIII) For that day's dainty timing I did botch.

VI.IX) Contra no-camp zoning, as had no hut,

VI.X) On dark Rangitoto, my pupils shut.

VII.I) Day two: I pack up at dawn, far away

VII.II) From that fairy boat's Rangitoto wharf,

VII.III) Upon which I just last morning did morph

VII.IV) Into an Australasian bushman. Lay

VII.V) Uncomfortably I did on thin mats,

VII.VI) Foraging for food on Pa-Hoy-Hoy flats.

VII.VII) Carib navy criminals' word "Ahoy"

VII.VIII) Now sounds logical, for I—too—said "Oy!"

VII.IX) Whilst dragging my body thru lava sharp:

VII.X) Particularly on stumbling I'd harp.

VIII.I) On pastoral plains of Motu-Taboo—

VIII.II) That murmur with prancing Pu-Kay-Ko Fowl

VIII.III) Who (mid-flap) thru-out mild,

           misty hills coo—

VIII.IV) I did not know of anybody's howl

VIII.V) In that country across from Toronto

VIII.VI) For or against how polls had to turn out

VIII.VII) Vis-à-vis that Whitish Habitation,

VIII.VIII) Which had to publish outcomings pronto

VIII.IX) So as not national souls to burn out

VIII.X) From constant, round-that-clock irritation.

XL

IX.I) Motu-Taboo was a naval station

IX.II) During World War Two, from Japan's gunships

IX.III) Guarding—with many an installation

IX.IV) Of military might—Auckland city.

IX.V) Britain's Pacific custodianships

IX.VI) Forgot Kiwi Country—itty-bitty

IX.VII) In contrast to London's nightly Blitz-Crag:

IX.VIII) Poisonous to Piccadilly's glitz-hag—

IX.IX) So Douglas MacArthur's army shows up

IX.X) And Tokyo's full invasion plan blows up.

X.I) Rambling amidst old cannons, cantinas,

X.II) I thought about national patinas

X.III) Atop this South Pacific Wondrousland

X.IV) For talking rabbit's Mad-Chai Party fit

X.V) Down dank, industrial kumara pit.

X.VI) Sang this sad song—"You, Too!"—
                    that famous band,

X.VII) South will go rising Singular Bush Hill,

X.VIII) At which, from Motu-Taboo, you may look.

X.IX) Pyramid-hill-top/coptic construction

X.X) Points skyward Khufu's lightning conduction.

XLIII

IV

KARANGA-HAPPY ROAD

I.I) That first Auckland day, Singular Bush Hill—

I.II) In smorgasbords of candy-cotton clouds

I.III) Floating thru many an idyllic thrill—

I.IV) Anything but vapid vistas to crowds

I.V) Could gift, from Mount Roskill to Okura.

I.VI) To Mount Hobson's Ora-Kay Basin by

I.VII) Ti-Ti-Kopu-Kay volcano sprinting,

I.VIII) Trains from Ponsonby to Papakura

I.IX) Pull up along Mangroving flats, hinting

I.X) At how iron howls turn harbour gulls shy.

II.I) Downtown's Connivingly Busy District:

II.II) Auckland CBD's traffic sign looks strict,

II.III) Full of Northland-bound, bluish-collar trucks

II.IV) Against bicycling accountants who hail

II.V) From Wist-Moor, Sandringham,

        or Grayish Lynn,

II.VI) Thru which winds Grand North Road

        —you lucky ducks—

II.VII) To Karanga-Happy Nightclubs. Don't bail—

II.VIII) You Māoriland youths—from vodka, rum, gin,

II.IX) Drunk by Long, Whitish Cloud Land's

        young adults,

II.X) All of whom join social alcohol cults.

III.I) In high school, as a solitary soul,

III.II) I did not party, and could hardly bowl.

III.III) Sans rap on my "Riting of Spring" playlist,

III.IV) I did not want to waltz thru JUULing mist—

III.V) Not that I had an invitation. Plus,

III.VI) Could not chant along if I had to cuss.

III.VII) Thus, my first youth cum alcohol party

III.VIII) Was in Māoriland, on Guy Fox Day (loud);

III.IX) Fancy liquors—tasting crisply tarty—

III.X) Got put in my hands by this rugby crowd.

IV.I) Karanga-Happy Road, which happy hour

IV.II) Always rings, shoots across motorway (dour)

IV.III) To Pitt Strait's bouncily barbarous bars,

IV.IV) Of dandily dashing daiquiri jars,

IV.V) By bankrupt, bacchanalian saunas

IV.VI) With primally yawping prima donnas

IV.VII) Who haunt baths ad infinitum, groping

IV.VIII) For any form of romantic hoping.

IV.IX) Sadomasochism is nightmarish,

IV.X) But snappily sold to minors—garish!

V.I) Middling, fiddling, diddling in cruisy clubs—

V.II) Which function as unsavory tub hubs—

V.III) Is sad, particularly for yauld youths

V.IV) Who know aorta-stability truths,

V.V) And start out loving, but finish cut out

V.VI) From matrimony's possibility,

V.VII) From which strong conclusion you must

butt out,

V.VIII) Pursuing random opportunity.

V.IX) Clubs ask youngins to party without pay,

V.X) As long as casual is what is gay.

VI.I) Won-sing upon a timing, Family Bar—

VI.II) Visitors vaporizing lungs of tar

VI.III) Torn in nico-tinny addiction—claims

VI.IV) Our world's most singularly grand nightclub

VI.V) Owing to global lockdowns. Smoking maims

VI.VI) Pulmonary parts thru fog; disco lights

VI.VII) Glow up a kid whom patrons call

        "Wolf Cub"—

VI.VIII) In front of gyrating artists with tights—

VI.IX) For parting from high school four months ago:

VI.X) Nonstop optimism his grinnings show.

L

VII.I) Mayhaps losing bits of purity with

VII.II) Ribald jigs on humid, dark dancing floors,

VII.III) Am told how virginity is a myth

VII.IV) That won't—for my body—crack any doors.

VII.V) Amidst Asian popular ballads now,

VII.VI) On black-pink masticating gum to chow:

VII.VII) All guys must bow to lubricant thrown out,

VII.VIII) For much is out of proportion blown out

VII.IX) Acquiring Human-Immuno-Virus.

VII.X) Condoms: almost as old as papyrus.

VIII.I) I do not know how, but I got working

VIII.II) For this saloon in which drugs go lurking.

VIII.III) As I did not at any point do drugs—

VIII.IV) In placing of which I fancy warm hugs—

VIII.V) I was most unusual pouring drinks

VIII.VI) Which I would not quaff on duty. My links—

VIII.VII) Luckily diaphanous—to brandy

VIII.VIII) Only aid my having fun. It's handy

VIII.IX) To run a pub without adoring port,

VIII.X) For tipsy bar-boys cut short: straight to court.

IX.I) Mixing Rasp-Airy chambords for Mai-Tais,

IX.II) On many occasions I say "Hi, Guys!"

IX.III) Various mouths slurp up var-mooth, bourbon:

IX.IV) Silly Curaçao punch I must curb in

IX.V) For hard, out-of-control, uncouth action

IX.VI) That you cannot allow to trick traction.

IX.VII) Imbibing shitty soju along scotch

IX.VIII) Indubitably brains bring down a notch.

IX.IX) To swallow swimming pools of brinkmanship

IX.X) Is not a way to build companionship.

X.I) That wintry August, got a girl from church

X.II) To accompany my optimism—

X.III) At which opportunity I will lurch,

X.IV) Insuring against most nihilism—

X.V) To drum-split "Dancing on My Own"

                soundtracks.

X.VI) Out-of-town guy on occasion asks, lax:

X.VII) "Is this a gay bar?"—whilst twinkling rainbows

X.VIII) Coat his skin in multicolour halos.

X.IX) Do I say how Karanga-Happy Road

X.X) Is happy? Should I show our cocktail load?

LV

V

WAILINGTON

I.I) On January's third-minus-first day

I.II) Hip hills I was hiking solitary

I.III) Around Wailington, towards Island Bay.

I.IV) Backpacking without books voluntary—

I.V) Apart from compact, bound biblical works,

I.VI) Pulpy pagination from which was torn

I.VII) In Tay-Waipounamu/South Island Kirks—

I.VIII) Lack of scholarly stimulus I'd mourn.

I.IX) Wandring thru third-minus-first-hand bookshops,
                    thus,

I.X) Sharp-shuffling I drift, so I would not cuss.

II.I) This city's Craftily Bawdy Domain:

II.II) CBD, holds out a Road of Cuba:

II.III) Cuba Straight, down which gay nightclubs complain

II.IV) About high costs. As dry as Aruba,

II.V) This walking-only way—Cuba Straight—cooks

II.VI) Quirky martial-arts marts and trading posts

II.VII) In caliginous paths of bricks, cracks, nooks;

II.VIII) Tourist trap haunting mansion attracts ghosts.

II.IX) Across from firms of naughty-nix knick-knacks

II.X) For copulation, I sift dusty racks.

III.I) Twiddling, fiddling thumbs across worn spinings,

III.II) In old-fashion, multicolour titlings,

III.III) Am missioning to find a folio

III.IV) That handicaps not as if polio—

III.V) Mayhaps fibrous-back—on aquatic trips.

III.VI) Ships from Wailington to Marlborough Sounds

III.VII) Zig-zag-zip atop tidal wavings—zounds!—

III.VIII) As if Pity Pan's bubbly companion:

III.IX) Tinkly-Kinky Bail, a fairy who blips

III.X) Not-at-any-point-land's canyon.

IV.I) As far away from London as a map

IV.II) Cartographically allows, most Magic,

IV.III) Not-at-any-point-land falls to my lap:

IV.IV) This scintillating South Island. Tragic,

IV.V) Only, is how I must wait to go back.

IV.VI) At a minimum, my soul shall switch tack,

IV.VII) Stop worldly affairs, hop on fairy boat—

IV.VIII) If multinational strip malls don't bloat—

IV.IX) To God's Country of Pounamu and Gold

IV.X) In which human spirits do not grow old.

V.I) In that Cuba Straight dollar library,

V.II) By fairy-dust-billow-stacks I tarry,

V.III) Until finally found for what I wish:

V.IV) Jack Caribou-Act's <u>On That Road</u>. To fish

V.V) For such a distinct publication,

V.VI) On such a spiritual vacation,

V.VII) In such contrary conditions, and win,

V.VIII) Is satisfying, similar to gin.

V.IX) Grinning, I paid for this classic story

V.X) As moving as vampiry films—gory!

VI.I) Triply-shot soy milk Flat-Whitish sipping,

VI.II) In cappuccino shop I sat ripping

VI.III) No-cost diagrams: diagonal trams.

VI.IV) Rufous railroads rock iron strings, as lambs—

VI.V) Whilst I part tipping—coat bucolic hills,

VI.VI) No itch for drug pills. Wailington's top thrills

VI.VII) Oft list such crimson, cabling carriaging,

VI.VIII) That harks to mountainous San Francisco—

VI.IX) Happily honors homo marriaging,

VI.X) Along disarmingly off-punk disco.

VII.I) Past Kiwi Country's capitol building

VII.II) Of gloss glass, plus corinthian gilding,

VII.III) In its mix of classical and young forms,

VII.IV) Am admiring history. Built on norms

VII.V) From Magna Carta, Māoriland's ruling

VII.VI) Political institution is strong.

VII.VII) Conical-hut politicians drooling,

VII.VIII) As if buzzing bugs—

       not from smoking bong,

VII.IX) From sugary, Manuka syrup (kiss);

VII.X) Bugs look bold, black, that colour of piss.

VIII.I) This banana-colour bug inhabits

VIII.II) Conical huts, waxing as if rabbits.

VIII.III) Apart from Himalaya-mountaining—

VIII.IV) Global glory for a knight-fountaining—

VIII.V) Sir Hillary took caring of such huts,

VIII.VI) From which his body got stung, but no cuts.

VIII.VII) No coconuts fall along that North Island;

VIII.VIII) Floral syrup flows from hippy highland.

VIII.IX) Pollinating Maui's south Valhalla,

VIII.X) Noir, balmy bugs chug syrup for challah.

IX.I) Kiwi country's capital construction

IX.II) Took nicknaming by this kind of bug's hut.

IX.III) Owing to Socialism's sour suction,

IX.IV) This round pyramid lulls, stuck in a rut,

IX.V) But still looks grand shut—tut!—as if a mutt.

IX.VI) A traditional, Anglo-Saxon wing

IX.VII) Jutts out from its cylindrical, young gut.

IX.VIII) Wailington's sophistication and bling

IX.IX) Surround slick masonry with Māori swirls

IX.X) Across from its bay that churns, swills, unfurls.

X.I) January's glowing, patch-coast of sands:

X.II) Bouncing, bumping balls; footprints, fading;

X.III) Many a pair of giggling, holding hands;

X.IV) Around I klutz, short in urban shading,

X.V) On my own in this wavy, windy town—

X.VI) But buoyant, bullish, laid-back, without frown.

X.VII) Lugging burst backpack to fairy boat dock,

X.VIII) Boarding I await on Albatross Rock,

X.IX) That sits—tidally—from a fountain tall

X.X) Which billows liquid into misty fall.

LXVII

VI

MARLBOROUGH SOUNDS

I.I) Shuffling atop slushy, salt-slippy stairs,

I.II) Aboard I shimmy, to find window, low

I.III) By acclivitous cliffs, swishing as hairs.

I.IV) Gladly am gawping; from limbo I go,

I.V) Dart down our fairy boat's cold, roomy hold,

I.VI) Atop Marlborough Sounds' misty sunlight,

I.VII) With frizzling fish and chips in tow. Am told

I.VIII) That this South Island wrought natural might,

I.IX) Which is ravishingly right. Mountains slip,

I.X) Marinading, to maritiming tip.

II.I) Firm foliaging drift down blush gumdrops;

II.II) Pinguinos plip-plap-plop as lollipops,

II.III) Dash across diving dolphins, fairy boats;

II.IV) Dinosaury flora flip down in moats.

II.V) South Island visitors pump Picton-wards

II.VI) For gazing highly unusual birds

II.VII) Who squak on glacial, South Pacific snows;

II.VIII) Viticultural Pounamu rock glows.

II.IX) Froth wonk woods fit for brachiosaurus;

II.X) Stripping aviary yawps sound porous.

III.I) Giddily, I alight at Picton's dock,

III.II) To many a kick-cooing Way-Ka cock,

III.III) Who—as joyful as Australasian clams—

III.IV) Fry fowl flavors as tasty as Tim-Tams.

III.V) Staid at Atlantis Backpacking that night.

III.VI) Amounting to a "Third-World Train Station,"

III.VII) This youth campground boasts Old Lady

cat plight,

III.VIII) Insofar as paws' multiplication

III.IX) Got too many a kitty; dank droppings

III.X) Coat avant-guard-dog murals in toppings.

IV.I) That matin, I paint toast with Mar-Might jam,

IV.II) In local fashion—not Viggy-Might sham;

IV.III) Do not fall for Australia's scam. Hop

IV.IV) To motorboat dock, swift-sailing to stop

IV.V) By historic bay, in which Captain Cook—

IV.VI) Many moons ago—lovingly did look,

IV.VII) To chart circuitous cartography,

IV.VIII) As scrupulous as hagiography.

IV.IX) Famous sojourn in this Marlborough bay

IV.X) Sounds placid—as avid, autumnal May.

V.I) Windily whips path thru mud, misty woods,

V.II) Full of sundry, biological goods,

V.III) From old timings that history forgot;

V.IV) Top-notch fossil scholars in shock got caught.

V.V) Long, Whitish Cloud Land shrubs

                sluggishly grow,

V.VI) In isolation. Many an odd crow,

V.VII) Halcyon hawk lost flight ability,

V.VIII) But not any falcon virility.

V.IX) Antipodal zoology astounds;

V.X) Thaumaturgical handiwork confounds.

VI.I) Toddling boy—four—asks:

       "Canst thou aid us, sir?"

VI.II) Murmur his vocal chords, mimic mild purr.

VI.III) Icy-landic, gray-bluish pupils point

VI.IV) To coastal cliff, with blond, gyrating joint.

VI.V) "What can I do?" Choking, says: "Just follow."

VI.VI) His punctuational twitch sounds hollow.

VI.VII) Curious, am trudging thru mulch, truss trunks,

VI.VIII) By Nordic kid of Titian curls, who plunks—

VI.IX) In panic—down twisty tussock of grass,

VI.X) Onto which grip taut hands of lanky lass.

VII.I) "Am about to fall off!"—hurls this poor girl.

VII.II) Knocking off knapsack, plunging I untwirl,

VII.III) To lift this four-plus-four-Augusts-old child,

VII.IV) Away from summit to aquatic wild;

VII.V) Panting along shrubs, this girl is gracious.

VII.VI) Without warning, local crowd forms

       —spacious—

VII.VII) From surrounds. Just four plus four plus

       four clans

VII.VIII) Inhabit this bay, with no asphalt plans.

VII.IX) Titular, triangular Christmas bush,

VII.X) Shadows many a swimming, splashing tush.

VIII.I) This propitious throng is introduction

VIII.II) To all broods in itty-bitty outpost:

VIII.III) Hardy muscularity induction.

VIII.IV) Youngins—by cozy gusts—host hoki roast.

VIII.V) Across Loch Ponga, this crisp, tranquil firth—

VIII.VI) Of Pinus-Phylum plants—

        sprouts, guffaws mirth.

VIII.VII) Flock fitfully disbands; singular boy—

VIII.VIII) With blazing, bronzish ring-lits—

        broadcasts joy.

VIII.IX) "Wouldst thou quaff a cup of oolong?"

VIII.X) To turn down said invitation is wrong!

IX.I) Follow him to his family's charming inn;

IX.II) Cicadas cuckoo cacophonous din.

IX.III) His kind, matriarchal kinswoman pours

IX.IV) Mug with ambrosial oolong. Kauri floors

IX.V) Support his sororal sibling, who blips

IX.VI) Jovially intoxicating trips.

IX.VII) Piwaka-waka birds plip-plap-plop yarns—

IX.VIII) Across from Arapawa Island barns—

IX.IX) Of living in this Pinus-Phylum town:

IX.X) Unsung cabochon, incants British Crown.

X.I) His patrimonial kinsman cuts cod

X.II) From trawling Upanishad-worthy rod;

X.III) Fulgurating rays romp; bopping boats blink;

X.IV) Rippling tidal thrusts rollick, wink.

X.V) Soul-warming, almost poignant in hindsight,

X.VI) This family hosts my body a fortnight

X.VII) In ancillary room. Mōhua rings,

X.VIII) Stirs aural organs at dawn; Hihi sings

X.IX) By barnacly planks, wharfs roughshod;

X.X) Jocund folks and I, Gurnard stocks maraud.

LXXIX

VII

TASMAN'S BAY OF GOLD

I.I) Aqua-mariny, Pill-Walrus Brook rolls

I.II) Thru Misty Mountains of Hobbits and Trolls.

I.III) Richmond Ranging Hills—rising up in rows—

I.IV) Rip triassic gills. Gnarly highs and lows—

I.V) Masticating mad-martian maroon rust—

I.VI) Thrust from Blin-Uhm to Graymouth:

Gold Rush bust.

I.VII) With Halving-Lock diplomats hitch-hiking,

I.VIII) From Picton I got to Canvastown's pub:

I.IX) Kiwi social hub. Now a pitch-viking,

I.X) Back-country soot dusts skin; I miss good grub.

II.I) In tramping shack, I dry off damp body;

II.II) Primordial paths twitch, grab ground shoddy.

II.III) Brick boots gush pools from stultifying rain:

II.IV) Clammy socks put walking-foot-warts in pain.

II.V) No road motor can putt out to this hut,

II.VI) In which I subsist by raisin, walnut—

II.VII) And that pasty gloop which pairs with
                    fruit jam:

II.VIII) Mucilaginous, tawny mush mauls yam.

II.IX) Illustrious, Illinois sandwich lunch;

II.X) Sun-dry mango; oats; cocoa—too—I munch.

III.I) Post many long days of constant hiking,

III.II) To rimy skinny-dips I took liking.

III.III) Two days' walk from road—

　　　　including crush rocks—

III.IV) Nobody shows up. I miss Bay-Gull Lox

III.V) From Totara-Nu-I: Woman King's

III.VI) Char-a-lot/Spamalot Sound: bay gulls fling

III.VII) Wriggling, wiggling fish atop trawling boat.

III.VIII) Just days ago, I slap on woolly coat

III.IX) To catch anything but sharks in Cook Strait

III.X) With oblong, frosty octopus as bait.

IV.I) My first occasion of truthful hauling

IV.II) Muscular dorsals with Māori calling,

IV.III) Thick fins from coral cornucopias,

IV.IV) I dig mauling salt-wall utopias,

IV.V) For nautically nourishing naval food,

IV.VI) That push olfactory buds to good mood.

IV.VII) Albatross pulchritudinously toss;

IV.VIII) Matriarchal, natural world is boss.

IV.IX) India-ink cod, rhubarb snaps I hoist,

IV.X) With tip-top grinding, apparatus joist.

V.I) Quotidianly supping fish and chips

V.II) As ambrosial as salt-tahini dips,

V.III) Sizzling Libyan pita, prick lava touch;

V.IV) Danish coil croissants—flaking—surpass Dutch.

V.V) Fujian chow-main stir-fry flips zucchini;

V.VI) Polish dumplings pop Sicily panini;

V.VII) Turkish ricing pilaf, China churros—

V.VIII) Piping-boiling food fantasy burrows

V.IX) Into throat that sucks cupboard cough candy,

V.X) Longs to scratch dry match: sounds

> highly handy!

VI.I) Pill-Walrus Brook banks bombard floral frills;

VI.II) Comfy cots dulcify sub-polar chills.

VI.III) To no avail, damp kindling am fiddling,

VI.IV) With many a moist, droopy match middling;

VI.V) Lugubrious logs lull; frumpy fronds fail;

VI.VI) Roof crack tick-tacks rain into puny pail.

VI.VII) Storm-drops blip-blop-blap à la raging raps;

VI.VIII) If only combustibility zaps

VI.IX) As rapidly as possum traps click-clack:

VI.X) Optimism floats off, ruffling kick-sack.

VII.I) Without warning, local guy kabooms fit

VII.II) Into fusty hut. On long-running sprints,

VII.III) This chap zips thru trails, taking from his kit

VII.IV) Matchbox for my kindling; I throw him mints,

VII.V) In thanks. This cordial Kiwi hints—

VII.VI) Scuffling across floor of vinyl and lints—

VII.VII) At my origin (pronunciation).

VII.VIII) I confirm in what country I was born:

VII.IX) On plains of Buffalo, Sioux tipis, corn;

VII.X) Doctor sighs, as if capitulation.

VIII.I) "What civilization day was thy last?"

VIII.II) "I now go having past thru urban fast

VIII.III) "For six plus six days, many a sun fall."

VIII.IV) Physician pulls air in and out of lung.

VIII.V) "Thy Washington Capitol—in a brawl—

VIII.VI) "Was burst into—bad! Trump's naming
was sung

VIII.VII) "By alt-right riot-ring instigators

VIII.VIII) "As horrifying as alligators.

VIII.IX) "Lots of photographs got hot on-lining

VIII.X) "Of vikings in hallow-halls con-mining."

IX.I) "Fuck… Did this law-slagging group

        carry arms?"

IX.II) "I do not know about furnishing guns,

IX.III) "But twiddling, twitting cyan bird alarms

IX.IV) "Now stop Donald Trump from

        publishing puns."

IX.V) I do not grasp much about this riot,

IX.VI) But this physician's account—I'll buy it.

IX.VII) My hiking portion is cut short,

IX.VIII) Short-cut Nail-son-wards: astir, lucid port.

IX.IX) Skip two days to Richmond farmland downhill,

IX.X) For sylvan dispatch information—nill.

X.I) Find full story in tranquil library;

X.II) Scoop moulds my political mood wary.

X.III) For calm, I hitch Takaka, Collingwood—

X.IV) By Holy Waikoropupu Hot Springs—

X.V) To Faring-Will Spit, Gold Bay, as I should,

X.VI) Whilst dismal, digital updating dings.

X.VII) Striding whimsical, Wharariki Rocks,

X.VIII) Hourglass to Puponga-position locks;

X.IX) Squalls grind crafts aground; sands silt
low-tiding;

X.X) Flying Dutchman Tasman floats to hiding.

XCI

VIII

ARTHUR'S PASS

I.I) His motor magnanimously blinks light,

I.II) Pulls across traffic, to my thumb's right.

I.III) Cantabrian plains—outskirts of Christchurch—

I.IV) Ravishingly roll round Rangiora;

I.V) Cymric mammal krill krick-crack Kaikoura,

I.VI) Simpatico South Island grand outdoors;

I.VII) Whaling Waipara wicks Waiau outpours,

I.VIII) To Bay of Flying, Albino Colt (lurch),

I.IX) From mythological Mount Olympus,

I.X) Gliding glad rainbows, gushing gild prim piss.

II.I) As windows wind down, sticky-bump signs show

II.II) Kiwi Antarctic affiliations:

II.III) McMurdo Sound, Victoria Land glow

II.IV) Ross Island, Scott Basing inclinations.

II.V) Having long stuck out burnt hand, am gracious

II.VI) To find a guy who looks non-pugnacious,

II.VII) Amiably asks of hitch-hiking goal:

II.VIII) "Am trying to go, without highway toll,

II.IX) "To Hokitika—art thou driving far?"

II.X) "I camp by Arthur's Pass; thou hit on par!"

III.I) With invitation, I happily hop

III.II) Into shot-gun; back by boot-trunk, bags drop.

III.III) <u>Glory Days</u>, <u>Lightning Road</u> riff sound pillow;

III.IV) Rippling radio kabooms <u>Born to Run</u>.

III.V) Bumptious ballads from Young Jar-Say billow

III.VI) Thru Plains of Rohan. I chomp hot-cross bun

III.VII) That this cordial chap of my aging bought;

III.VIII) His <u>Pink Cadillac</u> hand points to tan dot,

III.IX) As I'm going down badlands, lamb station:

III.X) Family land of Ngāi Tahu's nation.

IV.I) Mocha, pinot gris, chardonnay, damask—

IV.II) Anti-wintry auburns daub gusty hills;

IV.III) Vivifying drafts drill lungs sans a mask;

IV.IV) Southbound Alps uplift, swilling brumal chills.

IV.V) Choppy chip-chassis chuffs classic rock bard.

IV.VI) Hush-hush, cryptic/mystic, non-public yard—

IV.VII) Of botanic blooms—surrounds his dashboard.

IV.VIII) <u>Hungry Aorta</u> brims blood, kills cash-cord.

IV.IX) Around this glacial, national park

IV.X) I find my body dancing in that dark.

V.I) Am bracing my brain to ditch music rich

V.II) Of Boss Brucy: King who zings, clings,

　　　　　stains spring.

V.III) Cynical smog knocks most quality kitsch,

V.IV) Apart from Spring-Stain, who guffaws,

　　　　　gains bling

V.V) In bluish-collar, suburban fashion,

V.VI) With artistic, patriotic passion.

V.VII) William H. Taft's country sound-wavings

V.VIII) Flip flag-stars, pound pat global

　　　　　ground-pavings.

V.IX) Not at any point prior to this jaunt

V.X) Was hitch-hiking so wholly not in want.

VI.I) Sporty driving buddy and I fast switch

VI.II) Contact information. To him I pitch

VI.III) Writing papyrus mails cum postal stamps,

VI.IV) Amidst arduous, Arcadian tramps.

VI.V) Fast-forward six riotous months, show up

VI.VI) At his warm, Saint Albans habitation

VI.VII) Sans Dunny-Din's throw-up;

VI.VIII) Traipsing across Christchurch conurbation,

VI.IX) Us two romp thru Riccarton, Hillsborough,

VI.X) Bold bagpiping by Farm Park Scarborough.

VII.I) All is okay that will finish okay

VII.II) From suburban Ōtautahi that day.

VII.III) Chit-chat with Gandalf's stunt-doubling actor,

VII.IV) Who—for myrrhic, pyrrhic, occult factor—

VII.V) Chants Stratford-upon-Avon quotations,

VII.VI) À la drama, sans print-aid flotations.

VII.VII) Patchouli pulls <u>King John,</u>

<u>Sixth plus Sixth Night;</u>

VII.VIII) Danish and Scottish Kings kickify fight.

VII.IX) <u>Mid Post-Spring-Night's Fantasy,</u>

blabbing ass,

VII.X) <u>Much Ado About Nothing</u> polish brass.

VIII.I) Spicular wisps curl chin; vocal chords strum;

VIII.II) Old wizard wisdom thrills youths;

curtains hum.

VIII.III) At this Cornish guy's bookish bungalow—

VIII.IV) With Arthurian manuscripts aglow—

VIII.V) Driving pal and I thru film albums flip,

VIII.VI) Black and whitish prints whizz past at

blip-clip,

VIII.VII) Cataloguing plays from Brighton, Bristol;

VIII.VIII) Sir Ian photographs as if pistol.

VIII.IX) Crunching cinnamon biscuits,

swirl Whirl Gray,

VIII.X) On Anglia-azul China chai-tray.

C

IX.I) Back in Arthur's Pass, Kumara quidditch—

IX.II) That is, hitch-hiking—links lagoon with witch,

IX.III) Kicks mad-shift broom to Okarito, Ross;

IX.IV) For work: musty, arachnid-strand bathrooms

I floss.

IX.V) Ditch dark magic for mountainous hails;

IX.VI) Aspiring, Aoraki, Mount Cook try trails.

IX.VII) Hari-Hari hollows Whataroa;

IX.VIII) Wild Wanaka follows Makaroa.

IX.IX) Hill-billy Haast slows gastropod pacing:

IX.X) Total contrast to astro-rod racing.

X.I) Baby-boom, matrimonial pair took

X.II) My body to Wakatipu loch nook.

X.III) Woman-King's-Town luxury cocktails—

X.IV) Bought by kind hosts—I swig,

        glancing hawk-tails

X.V) That drift, sinuous, Wakatipu-ward.

X.VI) Hitch to Tay-Anau; squiz many a bird.

X.VII) Ginormous, Iris-bluish massif pond

X.VIII) Pounds minimalist camp: nocturnal bond.

X.IX) Again—in glacial, national park—

X.X) I find my body dancing in that dark.

IX

AKAROA

I.I) Lapis-lazuli harbour, crinkling, laps

I.II) Viscous tidal flats, turk-kois scallop caps.

I.III) Crackling, tawny bush, mahogany plains

I.IV) Carry Scottish lambs, Cantabrian grains.

I.V) Akaroa floats atop harbour long;

I.VI) Franco-Anglican church chiming ding-dong

I.VII) Shows historical, colonial past;

I.VIII) Blood-strands mix Māori-Gallo-British cast.

I.IX) Without clock-worry, Banks Half-Island rims

I.X) Tay-Waipounamu's shut, volcanic brims.

II.I) Nanto-Board-a-Lays company bought boat,

II.II) Many moons ago, to colony form

II.III) Antipodal South Island: Māori moat

II.IV) Had not by that hour sold out British norm,

II.V) But by arrival, colonists from Gaul

II.VI) Found Unifying Kingdom flags fly tall.

II.VII) Māori maharajahs in prior days

II.VIII) Did sign off South Island to royal rays

II.IX) Of Grand Britain's prickishly puissant crown

II.X) That still controls Australasian lands brown.

III.I) Luckily for said immigrants Gallic—

III.II) Plus a Bavarian family or two—

III.III) Local crown policy did not rollick

III.IV) Akaroa's founding. Command—boo-hoo—

III.V) Still rightfully staid in London's strong hands,

III.VI) But Norman-Aquitanian brass bands

III.VII) Burst out in symphony that blissful noon:

III.VIII) Pax Britannica to Paris was boon.

III.IX) Immigrants nail Alsatian constructions,

III.X) Farm Francization, British inductions.

IV.I) Akaroa's nasal surnamings mark

IV.II) Sangral origins from Joan of Ark's land:

IV.III) Autochthonous, florid, virgin bush park

IV.IV) Flumps atop mountains slipping into sand.

IV.V) To sparkling cyan, juts old-fashion wharf;

IV.VI) To tangoing hula skirts, flax fronds morph.

IV.VII) Crunchy wands of baking dough, snapdragons

IV.VIII) Align main road fit for Bilbo Baggins.

IV.IX) Fantastical, colourful townhousings

IV.X) Tally taut traffic, adorn pink blousings.

V.I) Oozy tidal ripplings plop against wall

V.II) Into which flour crumbs for quacking gulls fall.

V.III) Christchurch public library maintains post

V.IV) By fish and chips shop;

               from surrounding coast,

V.V) Hail copious, thalassic catch poolings:

V.VI) Waitangi Tribunal's lavish rulings.

V.VII) Cobbly-stony boardwalks skid past shopfronts;

V.VIII) Maritiming lions swim, giggling grunts;

V.IX) Dainty dolphins splish-splash, harbour spiking,

V.X) Nirvana panorama striking.

VI.I) By mini-gulf club, I waltz, thumb-strutting,

VI.II) As tan, blond kids guffaw, put-putting.

VI.III) Thumbs twofold switch in turns from
               solar pain;

VI.IV) Sunblock's gunky, mucoid armor was slain;

VI.V) Arm crawls across crisply sunburnt itch.

VI.VI) On damp, dusty folds, squint squiggly
               map glitch

VI.VII) That points thru hallow vistas, holy bays

VI.VIII) In which I would happily pass my days

VI.IX) For all of living by Franciscan ploy:

VI.X) Scintillating Iris salt-drops sob joy.

VII.I) Starting out from South Christchurch that matin,

VII.II) I wait by Hall's Wall Road shops of satin,

VII.III) As far away as any public bus will run.

VII.IV) For six nights prior, had lots of fun

VII.V) With caring family in Aranui,

VII.VI) As backpacking homo juris sui,

VII.VII) Am talking in Kaikoura to this kid,

VII.VIII) Who—my sororal sibling's sort—puts bid

VII.IX) With his matriarch for my fast staying

VII.X) Handful of nights on sofa sans paying.

VIII.I) Convivial kinswoman is so kind,

VIII.II) That I quickly got door combination—

VIII.III) "Go in/out at any hour, I don't mind,"—

VIII.IV) Without asking, to his habitation.

VIII.V) Ōtautahi's Avon Brook strut black swans;

VIII.VI) Solo, I plow unknown lands as if Hans

VIII.VII) In his Thousand-Annum Falcon (Star Wars),

VIII.VIII) Curiously crashing front stoops, bar doors.

VIII.IX) Aranui—majorly Māori folks—

VIII.X) Holds mossy graving-yards, Taka-Hay croaks.

IX.I) Back I stand by Akaroa's outskirts.

IX.II) Jalopy skids, parks; Irish lady blurts:

IX.III) "To what location art thou going now?"

IX.IV) "La Bons Bay." "Okay, hop in!"

"Thanks," I bow,

IX.V) Into this chassis with warm pair of twins

IX.VI) From County Galway. Knapsack pops on shins;

IX.VII) Colloquy flows. "How didst thou

pick this bay?"

IX.VIII) Lady asks, as windows wind humps of hay.

IX.IX) "La Bons Bay—Banks Half-Island's

most cut off—

IX.X) "Sounds glorious." As if Gandalf, blast off.

X.I) Dynamic Irish duo's motor falls

X.II) Thru rural idyll of shrill songbird calls.

X.III) To South Pacific, La Bons Bay brook spills—

X.IV) By bulls, adult lambs, alpacas on hills—

X.V) Tugs shrubby tororaro, rātā coast

X.VI) That blows chalky sand, Victorian ghost.

X.VII) Solicit strolling troop, who talk of farm

X.VIII) That might host work hands…

"Asking would not harm?"

X.IX) "Slán!" Irish twins shout by maroon mailbox;

X.X) Cum cocoa, I wait on crush-road-rocks.

CXV

X

LA BONS BAY

I.I) On July Fourth, I find my soul back,

I.II) By that mansion of many a knick-knack

I.III) On hand-paint, crimson kiosk driving-way

I.IV) In brilliantly brumal La Bons Bay.

I.V) First I visit this Land of Daffodils

I.VI) In January, without wintry chills,

I.VII) Thanks to that cordial pair of Irish twins;

I.VIII) Pinpoint rubicund barn built by swift Finns.

I.IX) Hop out, but no inhabitants abound;

I.X) Drafts sound as if nobody walks around.

CXVII

II.I) Atop Matagouri pond willows whoosh;

II.II) Lotus buds pop thru bog that cattails push;

II.III) Hara-kay-kay shrubs slip down hills,

zucchini plants;

II.IV) Cloaths-lining pins brandish Thai dying pants.

II.V) Yawping thru Nikau Palms, labrador hound

II.VI) Blithingly barks, pullulating bush bound,

II.VII) Disarmingly dowsing body in licks;

II.VIII) Saliva coats cowboy corduroy kicks.

II.IX) Sliding backpack hulk on ironwood porch,

II.X) Wiry twilight wisps blush horizon-scorch.

CXVIII

III.I) Put my mind to knock two jazzy doors down;

III.II) Unlatching lady brought my soul to town,

III.III) In yard of carrots, nasturtiums toiling;

III.IV) Pours Kiwi milk to cup: matcha broiling—

III.V) "That guy is so kind, ask to work for him."

III.VI) His pistons pump back prior to lights dim.

III.VII) Ask him if I could work for room and board—

III.VIII) Any task: shrub-trim, window-scrub,

                plug-cord.

III.IX) Kiwi quizzically asks:

                "Canst thou mow lawns?"

III.X) "But of coursing I can!"

                Background roam fawns.

IV.I) Patriarch-familias turns doorknob

IV.II) Of vino-fuchsia portal, glossy varnish,

IV.III) Untangling information about job

IV.IV) To undo unduly grown yard tarnish.

IV.V) Lawn-mowing is for this family—am told—

IV.VI) Unsavory task always put on hold.

IV.VII) Comfy curtains cut scholarly salon;

IV.VIII) Tumbling hardbacks swing-saw divan chiffon.

IV.IX) Chirpily look forward to cut crass grass,

IV.X) Praising tūmatakuru knolls thru glass.

V.I) British baking apparatus broils chips

V.II) From aromatic macrocarpa strips

V.III) Diffusing Scandinavian lodging.

V.IV) From popping-out attic stairway dodging,

V.V) Am shown to tippy-top floor window bunk,

V.VI) By Rastafarian rug, goat-skin trunk.

V.VII) By transpicuous silks, quasi-Amish quilts

V.VIII) Qualify my quill whilst squibbling on kilts:

V.IX) MacKinnon, MacNab, Urquhart tartans

V.X) Plait harmony, braid coo-cooing martins.

VI.I) Post-thorough-wash in palatian sauna,

VI.II) Thru which vitrails flit quirk avifauna,

VI.III) Drowsing I droop, on comfy pillows;

VI.IV) Cock that morn uproariously billows;

VI.V) Piquant Anathoth apricot jam toast

VI.VI) Wafts upstairs, tamarillo-guava roast.

VI.VII) Lawn-mow past passionfruit, citrus, squash:

VI.VIII) Roomy planation prolongs Macintosh.

VI.IX) Laundry from cords hang polychromatic

VI.X) On Kiwi manor aristocratic.

VII.I) As I tramp across Long, Whitish Cloud Land,

VII.II) Spasmodically fling back as glad farmhand

VII.III) To that hypnotic plot of La Bons Bay:

VII.IV) Prancing polka-dot appaloosas bray,

VII.V) Gambol by pīkao bush, stiff-stirrup;

VII.VI) Kākā, miromiro tomtits chirrup.

VII.VII) Ruby-maroon mailbox with kids' hand paint:

VII.VIII) Truthful compassion: optimally quaint.

VII.IX) Kūkupa pinions furiously flap;

VII.X) Kowhai boughs shadow, gloriously tap.

VIII.I) Luscious walnut/almond orchard tootling,

VIII.II) Macadamias I fast find pootling

VIII.III) Thru-out alfalfa-full daisy paddock.

VIII.IV) Nightfall's collation: crayfish and haddock.

VIII.V) From La Bons Bay lido, spin fishing craft,

VIII.VI) Put-putting along—

                    Twain's Tom saw your raft.

VIII.VII) Pilot by Banks Half-Island's coastal cliffs,

VIII.VIII) Snaring Kiwa's Moana-Nui stiffs;

VIII.IX) Haul aboard gargantuan crayfish tons:

VIII.X) Lip-smacking atop olivy oil buns.

IX.I) Riroriro grayish warbling rings toll;

IX.II) Currant-Goji dawn dusts galloping foal.

IX.III) Ticklish tauhou tintinnabulation

IX.IV) Tricks biotic consubstantiation.

IX.V) Auroral rays illumining gully

IX.VI) Astir stitchbirds. No pollutions sully

IX.VII) Chic chicory Chatham Islands Lily:

IX.VIII) Indigo indicatrix blooms frilly

IX.IX) Frisk crystal orchids, silly Saint John Worts.

IX.X) Ivory kōtuku in lagoon sports.

X.I) Bicycling past La Bons Bay library

X.II) Down tributary's road arborary,

X.III) Lolls historic church, basks rusty anchor;

X.IV) Kānuka burial ground sans rancor

X.V) Looms by ngutukaka, tōtara hurst;

X.VI) Llamas in babbling billabong curb thirst.

X.VII) On Whitmanian sod vibrato-loaf,

X.VIII) Praying for luxuriant autotroph.

X.IX) Lazing lambs land snugly; I miss my tramps—

X.X) Away from Adam and Ava's yard cramps.

CXXVII

XI

DUNNY-DIN

I.I) Drumkit cymbals, bass—punk rock music pounds

I.II) Mud backyard, nocturnally out of bounds

I.III) With pliant, prodigal sound injunctions

I.IV) That fail to monitor in dysfunctions

I.V) Chardonnay-chugging, cognac-glugging youths

I.VI) Who absorb by vomit alcohol truths

I.VII) Tripping on shards of sauvignon blanc vials

I.VIII) Which haul kiwi schoolboys and girls

        thru trials;

I.IX) Anybody living in Dunny-Din

I.X) Downs gin in dim, bibulous funny-bin.

II.I) Otago's most Brobdingnagian town,

II.II) Dunny-Din dons MacDougall's Pictish gown—

II.III) On Tay-Waipounamu's savannah fog—

II.IV) Built as amazing austral analog

II.V) To vicinal municipality

II.VI) Of Glasgow's stark originality.

II.VII) Stygian, Scottish masonry highlights—

II.VIII) Atop maudlin, sottish, blotto thigh-fights—

II.IX) Sooty plaza: outstanding octogon—

II.X) This oppidan pivot's odd polygon.

III.I) With many a woozy, sub-astral goul,

III.II) Notorious for its young adult school

III.III) Of post-high-school-instruction: Otago,

III.IV) Dunny-Din charms many an Iago

III.V) To chianti-quaff way youth in gala

III.VI) That mimics sub-lunary Valhalla

III.VII) Concocting wanton sybaritism

III.VIII) Mumbling crapulous primitivism;

III.IX) "Castling Strait" is voluptuary hub

III.X) Of Casanova pupils who club.

IV.I) Long, long ago living on Castling Road,

IV.II) In crimson-brick flat with cannabis load,

IV.III) Lots of fun I had, partying on rum;

IV.IV) Major major vodka disturbs young tum.

IV.V) Midnight moans out from window signal barf

IV.VI) That splats walkways in chunky, clarty scarf.

IV.VII) Parlour room rots in marijuana smog

IV.VIII) That studious, thrill-fun-loving guys hog;

IV.IX) Haight-Ashbury hippy souls fall soaring

IV.X) High across hillocks, Molly clouds snoring.

V.I) My initial, sapid introduction

V.II) To this South Glasgow's urban production

V.III) Was local lady, right of whom I sat—

V.IV) Whilst porting grossly ginormous straw-hat—

V.V) On Auckland-bound aircraft. Start discussion

V.VI) As wild as Rugby halfback concussion

V.VII) On politics, Waitangi, abortion,

V.VIII) Of which any philosophic portion

V.IX) Was broadcast to full flight.

    From Port Calm-Moors,

V.X) This Otago woman did unlock doors.

VI.I) Dunny-Din's capacious dock: Port Calm-Moors

VI.II) Runs bazooka that blams in twos and fours.

VI.III) I know, for I staid with this lady's clan—

VI.IV) On invitation—to cross-country plan

VI.V) In Ngāi Tahu/Northumbrian town small:

VI.VI) Otago's most imposing port of call.

VI.VII) Mastiff-dog-hiking on misty mud trails,

VI.VIII) Skip across dusty, rusty road of rails

VI.IX) That spurt pass motorway, biking path—

VI.X) Construction of which hails commuting wrath.

VII.I) Mounds of play dramas dot stucco casa

VII.II) In citron-sunlit tabula rasa;

VII.III) Paprika-pip-naan, coconut curry

VII.IV) Warm up amusing odors in hurry

VII.V) Atop sparkling Otago Harbourfront

VII.VI) Around which I slaggard-omnibus-bunt

VII.VII) To Māoriland's manic Larnach Manor

VII.VIII) That lifts atop Port Calm-Moors'

ship clamour.

VII.IX) In Wondrousland, fall down rabbit grotto;

VII.X) Botanical labyrinths mush mad motto.

VIII.I) Back on cosy Castling Strait that morning,

VIII.II) Dormitory wall cracks am adorning

VIII.III) With varicolour aluminum cans;

VIII.IV) Syrupy sapors shout from rug stain tans.

VIII.V) Folks rap, cannabinoid biscuit chomping;

VIII.VI) "No," I say to drugs whilst foxtrot-bomping.

VIII.VII) March with pals across whisky-cocoa toad:

VIII.VIII) World's singularly most angular road:

VIII.IX) Baldwin Strait, atop which am bagpiping;

VIII.X) Across mansions pitch-black am nag-griping.

IX.I) By sunlight, Kiwi constitution class

IX.II) I audit; by Sabbath-Day, sit on mass

IX.III) In draftily archaic, Gothic kirk

IX.IV) From which altars gargoyling moas lurk.

IX.V) In Australasia's most thorough bookshop

IX.VI) Thru atlas maps I gallivant; looks flop.

IX.VII) Obscurity's pulpy pagination

IX.VIII) Mirrors bookish and scholarly nation.

IX.IX) Hop past rococo train station on way

IX.X) To drink down iconic Saint Patty's day.

X.I) Saint Patrick's Day pardons lots of slurping

X.II) In town most partial (as is) to burping;

X.III) Māoriland's most profit-making drink shop

X.IV) Is Otago's Laith Liquorland fizz pop,

X.V) Outdoors of which I wait almost an hour

X.VI) To stock tall upon tiki soda sour.

X.VII) Crowds shoving into Dunny-Din's Woodstock

X.VIII) Pass us play ping-pong;

boys prank on good cock.

X.IX) Throw up I do not; in fact, flip my book,

X.X) Find pals with whom to play bishop and rook.

CXXXIX

XII

RAKI-URA STUART ISLAND

I.I) Waking up down in catamaran bunk,

I.II) Outdoors I find tidal standards sunk

I.III) Across from Codfish Island's hazy clouds

I.IV) That blot Raki-Ura in vigil shrouds;

I.V) Upstairs cook matin's brown sugary oats;

I.VI) Albatross caw-caws; ivory yacht floats;

I.VII) Stuart Island's diamond summits snowy

I.VIII) Mount sanctimonious sand banks doughy

I.IX) That hold nothing but Pīkao—not a soul;

I.X) Nobody will wash upon bashful shoal.

II.I) Raki-Ura floats south of Maui's boat;

II.II) Not a singular pig, possum, goat, stoat

II.III) Annoys avifauna on Stuart's Land.

II.IV) Biologically bizarro-odd strand

II.V) Of world's most titanic Kiwi bird ilk

II.VI) Out-count humans in Avalon of milk.

II.VII) This zoological Zion attracts

II.VIII) Cosmopolitan visitors, distracts

II.IX) Bounty nimrods from Oban's crackpot

II.X) Who inhabit bliss of bric-a-brac blot.

III.I) Mindfully milling about Milford Sound,

III.II) Fiordland I account as sacrosanct ground:

III.III) Fantabulous spot for matrimony

III.IV) Typify Shangri-La patrimony.

III.V) Mount Rahotu looms atop tidal marsh

III.VI) In which I find pink-purplish plastic harsh

III.VII) Which thru muck is fifty plus fifty bucks;

III.VIII) From Fiordland, hitch-hiking back on
                    camp trucks

III.IX) Past Mirror Loch, Boromir's canyon plains;

III.X) Kakapos cat-waul botanical strains.

IV.I) From Tay-Anau—graciously flush with cash—

IV.II) Go onto nirvana: rural road-trip bash;

IV.III) Past Taringatura, Nightcaps, Mossburn,

IV.IV) Southland inhabitants coast thru cross-turn.

IV.V) Rays Bush, Loch-Hail, Maka-Ray-Wa flow flux;

IV.VI) Pūtangitangi paradising ducks

IV.VII) Zonk Otatara, Awarua bogs

IV.VIII) Back of Invariably-Cargill's cogs

IV.IX) That spiral scorching-industry-fog punk;

IV.X) Bluff's forlorn coast drowns in thalassic junk.

V.I) Camp at Bluff Hill lookout in nylon shack

V.II) But matrinal drunkards rowdily quack

V.III) By World War Two barracks, dark sanctum crypt

V.IV) At two hours past midnight groggly off-script;

V.V) Dipsomaniacs shinny up rot roof

V.VI) Tumbling down to my tarp in grungy poof;

V.VII) Galvanic toy torch alights in panic

V.VIII) From squiffy barfly's attack satanic

V.IX) That luckily sparks no fatality;

V.X) "Sorry," says alcohol sodality.

VI.I) Bluff Hill floats atop South Island's south tip;

VI.II) Brisk fairy boats to Raki-Ura whip

VI.III) Amidst quasi-south-polar kahunas

VI.IV) To Wondrousland of mislaid lagunas.

VI.V) So charming that can upturn any frown—

VI.VI) Oban: Stuart Island's singular town—

VI.VII) For pub quiz is illustriously known;

VI.VIII) Down Halfmoon Bay, my trivial chip thrown.

VI.IX) In busy pub, my group almost wins clash;

VI.X) Dribbling pints of stout clarty barroom splash.

VII.I) Upon arrival to Oban I walk

VII.II) Sylvan footpaths across Kiwi bird flock—

VII.III) That, half-diurnal, yawp back-tingling howls:

VII.IV) Māoriland's most brilliant strain of fowls—

VII.V) To Anglican Church. (Was long ago shut.)

VII.VI) Thus, across itty-bitty Oban town I cut

VII.VII) To Scottish rust Kirk of Calvinism;

VII.VIII) Woman pastor proclaims humanism

VII.IX) As clamorously I unlock stuck bolt,

VII.X) Shocking Lilliputian parish with jolt.

VIII.I) Post-mass, talk with local dingbats, vicar,

VIII.II) All of whom I find at inn of liquor;

VIII.III) Loquacious, blond Auckland lady motions

VIII.IV) To adjoining Halfmoon Bay of potions

VIII.V) Buoyant in which bobs, coasts platinum yacht.

VIII.VI) "Dost thou know how to lash/bind/truss

knots taut?"

VIII.VII) Husband plus pal's circumnavigation

VIII.VIII) Of Stuart Island's magnification

VIII.IX) Was in want of sailors additional

VIII.X) To concoct victuals nutritional.

IX.I) Sailing past Waituna Bay's knobbly mists,

IX.II) Colossal crayfish I broil, wringing wrists;

IX.III) Mason Bay fans out in sand-shifting ritz;

IX.IV) Tūturiwhatu splits salt-liquid spritz.

IX.V) Panoply of podocarps, rimu bush

IX.VI) Harbour kākāriki; ruru owls hush;

IX.VII) Marauding mollymawks, mohua fowl

IX.VIII) Join Stuart Island Robins; kakas growl;

IX.IX) Mātātā frond-birds, saddling-back swallows

IX.X) Ally with tomtits, mask mataī hollows.

CXLIX

X.I) Primordial brooks by bluish cod drain

X.II) Harbour for Gorgon's Kid: matriarch slain

X.III) Via mirror, had ophidian locks

X.IV) That would turn onlooking souls into rocks.

X.V) Monstrous woman's child is bright colt

        with wings

X.VI) That fly across Hârâdwaith, Lord of Rings;

X.VII) Titanium alps loom top glaucous scrub;

X.VIII) Scrawny saplings Tarāpuka gulls rub;

X.IX) Port Pikihatiti rubbish constrains,

X.X) Multitudinous paradox contains.

CLI

XIII

CORMORANT-ILL HALF-ISLAND

I.I) Atop Waikato floats half-island strong

I.II) Of ill cormorant who cannot sing song:

I.III) Cormorant-Ill Half-Island holds hot coast

I.IV) Of salt lava liquids which fast foot roast.

I.V) Myth's Whitianga had his first landing;

I.VI) Captain Cook, his astronomic standing,

I.VII) In this kauri/kamahi woodland spot

I.VIII) Around which anti-buddhist brains rot:

I.IX) Cormorant-Ill Gold: sharp cannabis frond;

I.X) Many occupants of off-highs fall fond.

II.I) My first occasion of hitch-hiking falls

II.II) By Waikawau Bay; woman's motor stalls

II.III) Whilst tramping up podocarp plantation;

II.IV) Grimy window rolls, displays Caucasian—

II.V) Susurrus: "Wouldst thou fancy a lift?"

II.VI) Was told from childhood

        that hitch-hiking sucks;

II.VII) Maturity from humdrum wisdom plucks.

II.VIII) Across Mangōnui's magma road rift,

II.IX) Away in Northland, munch fish and chips

II.X) By Carry-Carry's Bay of Islands nips.

III.I) By Manawatāwhi, Triad of Kings

III.II) Point Rainy caps austral North Island springs;

III.III) Tramp down horizon that cannot finish

III.IV) Nor Long, Whitish Cloudland coast diminish;

III.V) Giant Sandhills roll into Pacific

III.VI) Far from any institution civic.

III.VII) Ahipara falls by Kaitaia hail,

III.VIII) Laughing, lazing on Araroa trail;

III.IX) Folks grow Mangamuka marijuana;

III.X) Floral child dropouts dial Dali-Lama.

IV.I) Waitangi kōkako Paihia purrs;

IV.II) Opua-Okiato fairy whirrs;

IV.III) Urupukapuka Island anguish

IV.IV) Floats Ngunguru, Waipu;

Poor Knights languish

IV.V) Right by Ruakākā, north Mangawhai,

IV.VI) Intoning: "Kia tau tō atawhai."

IV.VII) Tawharanui marks Matakana

IV.VIII) With many a varicolour canna;

IV.IX) Kawau Island floats by Warkworth, Sandspit;

IV.X) Pakiri dabchicks flip into hands mit.

V.I) Tiritiri-Matangi island flumps

V.II) Across Whangaparāoa runoff clumps;

V.III) Titipounamu, toutouwai robin,

V.IV) Tuatara lizards look pins bobbin;

V.V) Rotoroa and Rotorua mix

V.VI) Playing Tauranga's cartography tricks;

V.VII) Ngāruawāhia, Hamilton sink

V.VIII) Matamata's Hobbiton tourist rink;

V.IX) Ōpōtiki, Whakata-Nay Bays fall

V.X) Past Whakaari, Whitish Island's maul.

VI.I) Tikitiki tills Tokomaru Bay;

VI.II) Mangatuna, Makorori mould clay;

VI.III) Māhia Half-Island Nūhaka nicks;

VI.IV) Hastings, Motuku, Waipukurau kicks;

VI.V) South of Young Plymouth winds Whanganui

VI.VI) Black stilts Kakī, Kāmana drift on buoy;

VI.VII) Paraparaumu Kapiti Coast pulls;

VI.VIII) Pall-Murmurs Town North, Himatangi, Bulls

VI.IX) Float down to Porirua, Ōtaki

VI.X) Top Maunghakotukutuku rocky.

VII.I) Putauhina, Pohowaitai Islands

VII.II) Draping pallid Poutama highlands

VII.III) Sink past Kaninihi, Tomahawk Bays,

VII.IV) Murphy, Mokinui, Kaihuka Cays,

VII.V) Rukawahakura, Titi atolls,

VII.VI) Takiwi-wini, Toitoi point patrols;

VII.VII) To Ulva Island's Wharawhara sand,

VII.VIII) Dinghy atop rough Kapipi stand;

VII.IX) Gong-top liquid falls cascading spray-murk;

VII.X) Whitish tail stags gawk in patrician smirk.

VIII.I) Post-tracking-down godwit, kuaka spoor,

VIII.II) In Cormorant-Ill Half-Island I pour

VIII.III) Thru classic atlas of cartography

VIII.IV) Brims distinguishing logography;

VIII.V) Am loving this tiny-town of Coal-Vill;

VIII.VI) Tara-iti fairy fowl patrol hill

VIII.VII) By buddhist mahamudra unity

VIII.VIII) That attracts cannabis impunity;

VIII.IX) Many a hippy community gloats

VIII.X) Of hairy hashish and garrulous goats.

IX.I) Pals put forth invitation to potluck

IX.II) Far in Port Jackson's low-milliwatt muck;

IX.III) In district without Māori-British law

IX.IV) Adult lambs, hashish fans hack, puffing raw;

IX.V) Mootah miasmas malodorous stink;

IX.VI) Bolt outdoors, to calm companions I wink,

IX.VII) Waiting in orchard oratorical;

IX.VIII) Plush, apollonic plums historical

IX.IX) Imply that I should stay in nippy airs;

IX.X) Kauri trunks trip aromatizing stairs.

X.I) Auckland-wards from Whitianga I hitch

X.II) Saluting grand, triumphant country rich;

X.III) Maungawhau moulds Adam and Ava's yard

X.IV) British as Stratford-upon-Avon's bard;

X.V) Down sumptuous road pastoral: Coal-Dust-Sack,

X.VI) By Tudor villa bookish trunk I pack,

X.VII) In antiquarian Cymric cassocks,

X.VIII) Stuff bags with Woolf, Sir Walt-Air-Scott
                classics,

X.IX) Missing Country of Pounamu and Gold

X.X) In which human spirits do not grow old.

CLXIII

CLXV

Made in the USA
Monee, IL
26 August 2022

0f89407f-ce91-42c2-bedb-cacbc9368bacR01